CATS
BY MOTHER GOOSE

A LUCAS/EVANS BOOK

Lothrop, Lee & Shepard Books · New York

CATS
BY MOTHER GOOSE

SELECTED BY BARBARA LUCAS
PICTURES BY CAROL NEWSOM

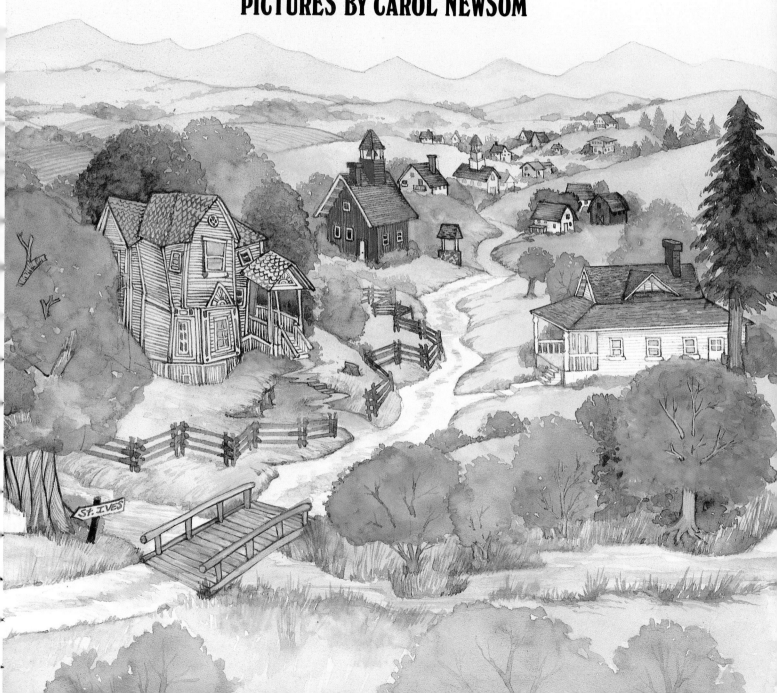

For two Margarets——my mother, Margaret Rider Lucas,
and in memory of
Margaret Carnegie Gauger——both great champions of Mother Goose

A LUCAS/EVANS BOOK

Text copyright © 1986 by Barbara Lucas
Illustrations copyright © 1986 by Carol Newsom
Printed in Japan.
First Edition

1 2 3 4 5 6 7 8 9 10

Library of Congress Cataloging in Publication Data
Mother Goose.   Cats by Mother Goose.
Summary: A collection of twenty-one Mother Goose rhymes about cats, including "As I was going to St. Ives" and "Ding, dong, dell, Pussy's in the well."   1. Nursery rhymes. 2. Children's poetry. [1. Cats—Poetry. 2. Nursery rhymes] I. Lucas, Barbara. II. Newsom, Carol, ill. III. Title. PZ8.3.M85
1986   398′.8   85-17053
ISBN 0-688-04634-7
ISBN 0-688-04635-5 (lib. bdg.)

Hey, my kitten, my kitten,
And hey, my kitten, my deary!
Such a sweet pet as this
Is neither far nor neary.

As I was going to St. Ives,
I met a man with seven wives.
Each wife and had seven sacks,
Each sack had seven cats,
Each cat had seven kits:
Kits, cats, sacks, and wives,
How many were going to St. Ives?

Jack Sprat
Had a cat.
It had but one ear.
It went to buy butter
When butter was dear.

Pussy cat, pussy cat,
   where have you been?
I've been up to London
   to look at the queen.

Pussy cat, pussy cat,
   what did you there?
I frightened a little mouse
   under her chair.

Pussy cat ate the dumplings,
  the dumplings.
Pussy cat ate the dumplings.
  Mama stood by,
  And cried, "Oh, fie!
Why did you eat the dumplings?"

Sing, sing, what shall I sing?
The cat's run away
   with the pudding string!
Do, do, what shall I do?
The cat has bitten it
   quite in two.

There was a crooked man,
    and he went a crooked mile,
He found a crooked sixpence
    against a crooked stile;
He bought a crooked cat,
    which caught a crooked mouse,
And they all lived together
    in a little crooked house.

Some little mice
    sat in a barn to spin.
Pussy passed by
    and popped his head in.
"Shall I come in
    and cut your threads off?"
"Oh! no, kind sir.
    You would snap our heads off."

The dog and the cat went out together
To see some friends just out of town.
Said the cat to the dog,
"What d'ye think of the weather?"
"I think, ma'am, the rain will come down.
But don't be alarmed,"
Said this amiable fellow,
"For I have an umbrella
And it will shelter us both."

Dame Trot and her cat
Sat down for a chat.
The Dame sat on this side
And puss sat on that.

"Puss," says the Dame,
   "Can you catch a rat
Or a mouse in the dark?"
   "Purr," says the cat.

I like little Pussy,
   Her coat is so warm,
And if I don't hurt her,
   She'll do me no harm.
So I'll not pull her tail,
   Nor drive her away,
But Pussy and I
   Very gently will play.

Ding, dong, bell,
Pussy's in the well!
Who put her in?
Little Johnny Lynn.
Who pulled her out?
Little Tommy Stout.
What a naughty boy was that,
To try to drown poor pussy cat,
Who never did him any harm,
And killed the mice in his father's barn.

Pussy cat sits by the fire,
How can she be fair?
In comes the little dog,
"Pussy, are you there?
How do you do, Mistress Pussy?
Mistress Pussy, how d'ye do?"
"I thank you kindly, little dog,
I fare as well as you!"

Pussy cat Mole
jumped over a coal
And in her best petticoat
burnt a great hole.
Poor Pussy's weeping,
she'll have no more milk
Until her best petticoat's
mended with silk.

Pussicat, wussicat, with a white foot,
When is your wedding, for I'll come to it.
The beer's to brew, the bread's to bake,
Pussy cat, pussy cat, don't be too late!

Puss came dancing out of the barn
With a pair of bagpipes under her arm.
She could sing nothing but fiddle-de-dee,
The mouse has married the humble bee.
Pipe, cat—dance, mouse—
We'll have a wedding at our good house!

Double Wedding at the home of Mother Goose

The cat sat asleep by the
   side of the fire,
Her mistress snored loud
   as a pig;
When Jack took his fiddle,
   by Jenny's desire,
And struck up a bit of a jig.

Three little kittens
They lost their mittens,
    And they began to cry,
"Oh, mother dear, we sadly fear
    That we have lost our mittens."
"What! lost your mittens,
You naughty kittens!
Then you shall have no pie."
"Mee–ow, mee–ow, mee–ow."
"No, you shall have
no pie."

There once were two cats of Kilkenny,
Each thought there was one cat too many,
So they fought and they fit,
And they scratched and they bit,
Till, excepting their nails
And the tips of their tails,
Instead of two cats, there weren't any.

The two gray kits
And the gray kits' mother,
All went over
The bridge together.
The bridge broke down,
They all fell in.
"May the rats go with you,"
Says Tom Bolin.

Hey diddle, diddle!
The cat and the fiddle,
The cow jumped over the moon.
The little dog laughed
To see such craft,
And the dish ran away with the spoon.